COLLEGE WRITING PROGRAM

Jeffrey Carman

Kendall Hunt
publishing company

Cover image © Shutterstock.com

www.kendallhunt.com
Send all inquiries to:
4050 Westmark Drive
Dubuque, IA 52004-1840

CONTENTS

SESSION ONE

1. Welcome! We're glad you're here!

    A. Why we're here—to IMPROVE your writing!

    B. _____

    C. _____

    D. _____

    E. _____

    F. _____

    G. Classroom rules and standards of behavior

2. Origins of the PRIME Writing Program:

    A. A State University level

    B. Help for students to SUCCEED

    C. Results

3. SO LET'S GET GOING!

    A. A show of hands….

    B. CLASS ACTIVITY:

    1. _____

    2. _____

    3. _____

    4. _____

    5. _____

4. Goals of this course:

    A. Better understanding of the writing process

    B. Less fear of writing / gain more confidence

    C. Learn and practice how to keep a class journal

    D. Learn approaches to common writing problems

    E. Review basic components of a good essay

    F. Get an idea of academic expectations in college

    G. Produce a finished essay in proper form:

    1. Go step-by-step through the writing process

    2. Gain better understanding of concepts

    3. It's good practice for you

5. Writing Strategies—getting started

   A. Brainstorming

      1. Cloud clustering

      2. Freewriting

      3. Making a list of thoughts or ideas

   B. Outlining

      1. For good flow of ideas

      2. For organization

6. Writing project for this course. Expository writing

   A. Used a lot: _____

      1. The word Expository means: _____

      2. Our project for this course: _____

      3. Length when finished: _____

      4. Other info: _____

          _____

          _____

7. Our writing assignment for this course: Explain a Process

   A. Step one: choose a process

      1. Something you already know how to do

      2. Something with specific STEPS leading to a GOAL

      3. Pick something you like to do or are interested in: it's no fun writing about something you hate

   B. Advice about what NOT to choose:

      1. NOT too simple—don't choose "How to Open a Can of Pepsi"

      2. NOT too complex—don't choose something with too many steps—you only have four pages maximum for the entire essay

      3. NOT too general or basic—"How to make scrambled eggs" is not very interesting to the reader

      4. NOT too physical—"How to do a triple somersault reverse flip on a half-pipe" will be too hard to explain in words alone—the average reader will not understand

      5. NOT too creative—with artistic or creative activities, everybody has their own way, so one explanation doesn't work

      6. Process having to do with computers or other electronic devices should be avoided: they often have steps that involve following prompts, so an explanation essay like the kind we're writing doesn't work well; it's boring just following prompts

      7. Some processes relating to work or a job can be good topics, but be careful; if a step in the process is done a certain way because "We've always done it that way," or "Because the boss says so," that is NOT a good topic for your explanation essay

      8. RECIPES can be good topics, but the essay has to include explanations, so a recipe off of a box from the store is not a good topic for this project

8. Keeping a Journal

   A. Very common in college English classes; also used in_____ in college

   B. One journal is due each session—it is due at the_____ of class each day

   C. $\frac{1}{2}$ to $\frac{3}{4}$ page _____; write neatly and legibly

   D. For this course: we want your _____ about the course and what we did in that day's class session:

      1. What you thought about the program that day

      2. Anything that stood out to you

      3. Did you LEARN anything about writing that you didn't know before?

      4. Which BRAINSTORMING technique seems the most useful to you?

9. Homework for next time:

   A. Journal—discuss #1 – #4 above in your journal.

   B. Journal due at the START of class

   C. THINK about the TOPIC you will choose for your Explain a Process essay—we will discuss it MORE next time

SESSION TWO

10. Welcome Back!

    A. Journal is due

    B. Go over journal—class exercise:

        1. Proper length? $^1/_2$ to $^3/_4$ page handwritten

        2. Is writing LEGIBLE?

        3. Is journal on-track?

            a. Review 9A #1 – #4 on previous page—does the journal discuss these things?

11. Our writing assignment for this course:

    A. Explain a Process—class activity:

        _____

        _____

        _____

        _____

        _____

    B. THINK about your topic—you need to DECIDE today at the end of class

12. Annotating and note-taking: use a winning strategy

    A. In your textbooks: Highlighting, underlining, or note-taking—which way is best?

        1. In high school: _____

        2. In College: _____

    B. How many notes should you take?

        1. From lectures:

            a. Of course you can take NOT ENOUGH notes

            b. But can you take too MANY notes?

            c. Question for the class…

                1. _____

                2. _____

                3. _____

                4. _____

        2. Taking notes from the board or PowerPoint presentations:

            a. Most stuff on the board is _____, or it would not be put on the board!

            b. Don't take TOO many notes during PowerPoint; it's better if you _____ in class and get the flow of ideas, so do NOT get bogged down in details

    c. If you have been keeping up on assignments, you should know if the material in the PowerPoint is also in the book—if it is, your notes can be _____intense and thorough, and you can concentrate on the _____of the presentation

C. Where should you write your notes?

    1. Notebooks are best:

        a. _____

        b. _____

    2. Writing in textbook margins should ONLY be _____ _____ or _____ _____:

    3. Longer notes should NOT be put in the textbook; put longer notes in _____ _____, where they BELONG.

D. SUMMARY of note-taking advice:

    1. Not too _____and not too _____

    2. Focus on the _____ideas or concepts

    3. Write only keywords or short key phrases in margins of textbook: for longer notes, use a notebook

    4. In college, use a separate notebook for _____

    5. Use a different _____for each notebook, so you don't get them mixed up when you are in a hurry someday.

    6. Highlight or underline—once you're in college, you _____ the books, so it's up to YOU how to mark them!

        a. But choose one method and stick with it—DON'T mix and match highlighting and underlining, because it will be confusing later

13. Our writing project: "Explain a Process"

A. Officially choose your process and write it here: _____

B. Be ready to say what your process is when we go around the class

14. Homework for next time:

A. THINK about your process

    1. Think about the things NEEDED to complete your process

    2. Think about the STEPS in your process—in proper order from start to finish

B. Journal: discuss: is the note-taking advice you learned today HELPFUL?

SESSION THREE

15. Welcome Back!

    A. Journal is due

    B. Go Over journals—class exercise:

        1. LEGIBLE?

        2. Proper length—$^1/_2$ to $^3/_4$ page handwritten

        3. Is journal on-track and THOUGHTFUL?

            a. REVIEW question in B on previous pages—does the journal DISCUSS it clearly?

16. Reading for Understanding

    A. In college, you are going to be doing a _____

        1. NOT just in your English classes

        2. ALL academic disciplines emphasize reading and writing in order for students to _____

        3. Even _____ schools require a lot of reading from their students

    B. Often, the material you read will be_____ and confusing

17. Different readings will present opposing views on the same subject

    A. Opposing positions will both have good points to make

        1. At some point, you will be asked to take a position on the subject and write about it

        2. If there is no "right" or "wrong" position, how do you decide what position to take?

        3. There is a technique that WORKS to help you with this type of reading. It is called:

            Reading _____ and _____ the _____

    B. This is a way of reading that really HELPS TO:

        1. Focus your ideas

        2. Weigh different positions

        3. Decide where _____ stand on controversial issues

    C. Reading with and against the grain:

        1. Reading WITH the grain: First, read the passage or selection _____

            a. Agree with assertions and conclusions

            b. Don't challenge assumptions; accept them

            c. As you read, _____ your head whenever you can

        2. Reading AGAINST the grain: second, read the passage or selection AGAIN, but this time, you are_____

            a. Be skeptical and unconvinced

            b. Challenge all facts and statistics

            c. Question all conclusions

            d. As you read, _____ your head whenever you can

3. Third, you need to _____ about the two ways you read the passage or selection:

    a. What main issues or arguments become apparent by the two different ways of reading?

    b. Which way of reading is "better" or "more_____" for you?

    c. Are there any arguments or assertions that now appear unfair or foolish?

    d. Are there any arguments that now appear particularly persuasive to you, even under close scrutiny?

    e. Do the strengths and weaknesses of the author's points seem clearer to you now?

4. Now here is NEWS about this technique; there is good news and bad news

    a. The good news: _____

    b. The bad news: _____

D. Making Lists of Pros and Cons

    1. Can help sort out complex issues

    2. Make FOUR lists to compare the points that are being made:

        a. Points for

        b. Points against

        c. Arguments or rebuttals to the points for

        d. Arguments or rebuttals to the points against

E. "Scale of Justice" method of determining the value of arguments:

    1. Not all points made for or against an argument are equal in weight or power

    2. Assign specific "weight" to the points made on each side, then see how they stack up to each other when they are compared on a "scale"

18. Homework:

A. Make a LIST of All the things needed to complete your process—okay to use bullet points

B. Make a LIST of the STEPS in your process—in proper ORDER from start to finish—okay to use bullet points

C. Journal–discuss:

    1. Have you heard of Reading With and Against the Grain before?

    2. Does it seem like a USEFUL way to sort out controversial issues?

    3. Do you intend to TRY it?

SESSION FOUR

19. Welcome back!

  A. Journals are due

  B. Go over journals—class exercise:

   1. Is the journal ELIGIBLE?

   2. Did they discuss numbers 1→3 on previous page?

  C. Conclusions about Reading with and Against the Grain:

   1. _____

   2. _____

   3. _____

20. Essay Construction—the three main parts of an essay:

  A. Introduction

   1. ALWAYS is the _____ paragraph in the essay

   2. Usually just one paragraph in short essays—a short college essay is five pages or less, double—spaced

   3. The intro should start with a general statement about the topic—it should _____ the topic to the reader

   4. The intro must include the main idea of the essay: this main idea is called the _____

    a. Also sometimes called the controlling idea of the essay

    b. The rest of the essay supports and refers to the main idea

    c. The thesis MUST be in the introduction, usually as the last sentence of the intro

  B. Body

   1. Explains and supports the thesis

   2. Must have clear and organized flow of ideas

   3. Must be divided into proper paragraphs

    a. Each paragraph in the body offers specific support for the thesis

  C. Conclusion

   1. Signals _____ of the essay

   2. The conclusion is NOT _____; it does NOT repeat points that you have already made

   3. There is NOTHING wrong with using the phrase "_____" at the start of the conclusion—it is ACCEPTABLE college-level construction

   4. Using that phrase is GOOD because it lets the reader know _____ _____

   5. The conclusion should echo the _____ from the intro and _____ _____

6. Think of ending your essay the way you would _____ :
not too abrupt, but don't linger or stall either

21. Types of Writing—Part One:

   A. Expository Writing: expository means _____

      1. Used in college a LOT: it's ESSENTIAL to success in college

      2. Shows others what you know

      3. "How to" writing is very common in this category

      4. Makes a good project for this program

   B. Persuasion and Argument

      1. Three modes of persuasion, according to Aristotle:

        • _____

        • _____

        • _____

   C. Persuasion used in Advertising

      1. Class activity: Ads we discuss in class:

Commercial or ad:	What is the intended reaction?	Which mode is being used?
_____	_____	_____
_____	_____	_____
_____	_____	_____

      2. Summary of advertisement and marketing:

        a. These three modes of Persuasion can be very _____

        b. You may not always _____ of the effects that advertising has
   on you

        c. Learning more about persuasion and argument can help you _____ yourself
   from manipulation.

22. Your essay Project: Explain a Process:

   A. Peer editing—trade papers

   B. List of things needed to complete the process—CHECK THESE:

      1. Bullet points / easy to read

      2. Clear and organized?

      3. Does the list appear to be COMPLETE?

   C. List of STEPS in the process—CHECK THESE:

      1. Bullet points / easy to read

      2. Steps in proper ORDER from start to finish

      3. Steps clear and organized?

23. Explain a process essay

   A. What is next:

      1. In between the steps, add EXPLANATIONS for each step:

         a. Advice or insider's tips

         b. Why the step is done that or why now

         c. Encouragement; keep the reader interested

         d. Tell the reader what to expect when they do that step

         e. Negative advice: _____

         f. Warnings; tell the reader what is needed for safety, but be positive; don't _____ the reader about the process

         g. Anything else the reader needs to know

         Think about the _____ of the process; all of your steps and advice should be in that direction

      2. To start your essay, it needs a proper _____

         a. ONE paragraph at the _____ of your essay

         b. FIVE TO SEVEN lines, TYPED and _____

         c. Start with a _____ statement about your subject: one two sentence or so

         d. Move to a _____ statement about your subject in the next sentence

         e. The last sentence of your introduction should contain the _____

         f. The thesis should specifically refer to _____ of your process

         g. Type your intro in proper essay from:

            1. Put your name, class, and date on it as we discussed in class today

            2. Put a good TITLE at the top

24. Homework for next time:

   A. Explain a Process essay:

      1. Take your list of STEPS and add ADVICE in-between each step—just one sentence or two for each step—follow GUIDELINES on page 27

   B. Write your Intro Rough Draft—follow GUIDELINES on previous page

   C. Journal: discuss:

      1. Do you understand the three modes of persuasion: Ethos / Logos / Pathos?

      2. Are you going to WATCH how they are used to try and persuade you?

      3. Have you used Peer Editing before?

      4. Does the Peer Editing HELP you with writing a BETTER essay?

SESSION FIVE

25. Welcome back!

    A. Journal due—review:

        1. Is journal LEGIBLE?

        2. Does journal discuss the questions on previous page part C?

        3. Is the journal THOUGHTFUL?

26. Explain a Process essay

    A. Peer Editing

        1. Take your list of STEPS with ADVICE in-between—TRADE with another student

        2. REVIEW the advice in-between each step

            a. Does the advice make SENSE?

            b. Does it help EXPLAIN that step?

    B. Intro Rough Draft:

        1. Turn it into your Instructor—they will review it and return it to you next session

27. The CORE of your essay—or _____ essay: the _____

    A. Should be CLEAR and _____

    B. Should be at the _____ of the intro—the LAST _____

    C. Will be _____ by everything else in the essay

    D. Normally, the thesis will be _____ sentence

    E. For your essay Explain a Process:

        1. A _____ thesis

        2. "By following these _____,"

        3. Then state the _____ of your process

28. Types of Writing—Part Two:

    A. Creative Writing: expressing yourself

        1. Creative expression of thoughts and feelings and ideas

        2. Examples of creative writing:

        _____

        _____

        _____

        3. A good way to "let it out": can help with CATHARSIS, which means _____

        _____

B. Remembrance—helping the reader to _____

    1. Works well for profiles of peoples, places, historical times, and so forth.

    2. Often uses narration—tells a _____ to help the reader understand

    3. Includes _____ DETAILS to help the reader see and feel

    4. Can be meaningful and moving to readers

C. Analysis—studying something for a specific purpose:

    1. Involves consideration of _____

    2. Involves _____ and looking for answers

    3. May involve considerations of alternatives

    4. Examples in high school or college:

        a. Personal: _____

        b. History class: _____

        c. Computer class: _____

D. Evaluation—determining the VALUE of something

    1. Stating the quality of something: _____

    2. Justifying the position taken

    3. REVIEWS are a common form of evaluation:

        a. _____ reviews on TV

        b. _____ reviews online

        c. _____ reviews in a consumer magazine

        d. _____ in car magazines

E. Persuasion and Argument—Some final thoughts:

    1. An important topic

    2. Our discussion of modes of persuasion is only barely scratching the surface of this subject

    3. In college, these issues are discussed in _____

29. Why Writing Matters:

A. Writing well improves your _____

B. Improves your _____ with others

C. Writing fosters _____ and satisfaction

D. Class activity:

    1. _____

    2. _____

    3. _____

    4. _____

    5. _____

    6. _____

30. Homework for next time:

    A. Your essay Explain a Process:

        1. REVIEW your STEPS and ADVICE in-between your steps—make sure you didn't leave anything OUT

    B. Journal—discuss:

        1. Is Peer Editing getting more comfortable for you?

        2. Is Peer Editing HELPING you write a BETTER essay?

        3. Are you clear about the THESIS:

            a. Where it goes in the essay

            b. States the MAIN IDEA

            c. Is SUPPORTED by the rest of the essay

            d. Your thesis is "By following these steps…" then state GOAL of your process

            e. Are you INTERESTED in creative writing? How you ever written a poem or short story? TRY IT!

SESSION SIX

31. Welcome Back!

    A Journal due—review:

        1. Is journal LEGIBLE?

        2. Does journal discuss the questions on previous page part B?

32. Essay project—Explain a Process:

    A. Your essay needs a conclusion

        1. After your process is over, your ESSAY needs to be _____

        2. Your conclusion should start by echoing the _____: say it in other words

        3. Do not _____ in the conclusion.

        4. Just wrap it up with some _____ thoughts

        5. Congratulate the _____ for completing the process successfully.

        6. It is OKAY to start your conclusion with the words _____: it SIGNALS to the reader that the essay is almost over.

        7. No new ideas in conclusion

33. Purpose and Audience

    A. Whenever you are writing ANYTHING:

        1. Keeping the PURPOSE of your writing in mind is _____

        2. Writing can have various purposes:

            a. To _____

            b. To _____

            c. To _____

            d. To _____

            e. To _____

            f. Some writing can have _____

        3. _____ of the essay should be in support of the purpose

    B. Audience

        1. Remembering the audience is _____ to keep in mind whenever you are writing _____

        2. Your audience can _____; therefore:

            a. Pay attention to the needs your specific audience

            b. Stay true to your thoughts, but adjust to your audience as needed

3. WHO is your audience in academic writing?

    a. _____ adults

    b. _____; writing in other countries is different

    c. _____ people with common knowledge and generally accepted beliefs

4. Class activity

Type of writing:	Purpose	Audience
Note to your teacher about why you were late to school	_____	_____
Funny postcard from your vacation that you send to a friend back home	_____	_____

34. Language and Tone:

  A. Language

    1. _____ to keep in mind in your writing

    2. Can vary in some types of writing:

      a. Based on purpose and audience

    3. For academic writing, language is very specific:

      a. Do NOT speak directly to the reader

      b. Do NOT announce what the paper is going to discuss

      c. The essay has its OWN VOICE

    4. No use of _____ words in an academic essay

    5. No _____—EVER! Unless you are quoting someone EXACTLY, avoid all curse words—even if you are quoting, try to avoid it; find another quote that makes the same point without profanity

    6. No abbreviations or other words like you use in texting

  B. Tone

    1. The tone of your essay is _____ to keep in mind in your writing

    2. Can vary in some types of writing:

      a. Based on purpose and audience

    3. For academic writing, tone is very specific:

      a. Stay _____ and _____, but not fancy or wordy

      b. Avoid _____ tone or phrases; take your assignment seriously

      c. Do NOT be _____ in college essays; some people do not understand or like it

  C. Class activity: Two letters that you are going to write:

    1. Letter one: A typed letter that is going to be mailed to a friend of your father, asking about the possibility of him giving you a job in his company over the summer:

    Language: _____

    Tone: _____

    2. Letter two: An email to a cousin or friend who lives in another town and is the same age as you are, telling him or her about your time in college so far:

        Language: _____

        Tone: _____

35. SUMMARY of purpose / audience / language / tone:

    A. They are all _____ with each other

    B. They are all _____ in your writing

    C. They should _____ be kept in mind whenever you are writing _____

36. Homework for next time:

    A. Explain a Process essay

        1. Write your CONCLUSION

            a. Follow Guidelines on section 32 and Appendix page 27

    B. Journal—discuss:

        1. Are you CLEAR about what the conclusion does—echo thesis and wrap it up?

        2. Are you CLEAR about what the conclusion does not do–No summary–No new ideas?

        3. Are you OKAY with using "In conclusion" to SIGNAL to the reader?

SESSION SEVEN

37. Welcome back! We're making progress now!

    A. Journal due:

        1. Is it LEGIBLE?

        2. Does it discuss the questions in Section B on previous page?

        3. Is it CLEAR and THOUGHTFUL?

38. Explain a Process essay:

    A. It's time to create the _____

        1. Put all the pieces _____:

            a. Introduction

            b. Thesis statement—at _____ of intro.

            c. List of _____ needed to complete the process

            d. The STEPS in your process—in clear _____ from start to finish

            e. ADVICE in–between the _____: to _____ the process to the reader

            f. The CONCLUSION—to wrap up and finish the essay on a _____ note

39. Success in college—to SUCCCEED in college, you need:

    A. Proper ATTIUDE and good HABITS:

        1. You need to take college _____

        2. You need to think of college as an _____:

            a. An investment in _____

            b. An investment in _____

        3. THINK about the REASON you are in college:

            a. So you can graduate from college with good _____

            b. To get a good job and start a rewarding _____

            c. To earn a decent salary and have a good _____

    B. Class behavior:

        1. Proper attendance is _____ in college

            a. You should make strong efforts to attend _____ class every time

            b. You should always be _____ to every class session–NEVER be _____

            c. If you are going to be late to a class, you should still _____ to show the instructor you tried and to still get what you can out of that class session

            d. If you miss a class, you should contact the _____ to find out what you missed, what you need to do to catch up, and how to get ready for the next class session

2. If you know an answer in class when the teacher asks, you should _____

3. If the instructor puts something up on the board or projected on the screen, that means that it is _____

40. _____ assignments are IMPORTANT in college

   A. When instructors give out homework, they EXPECT it to be _____ by the time it is due

   B. Instructors in college will not tolerate or accept _____ for not doing homework

   C. In college you will be doing a lot of _____

   D. You will have READING to do _____ after class—sometimes for every one of your classes

   E. You will not have _____ to read everything multiple times—so you have to read EFFICIENTLY:

      1. Use ANNOTATING—like we went over in Session 12

      2. Pre-read a chapter BEFORE you actually read it—this is called _____:

         a. Read the title, headings and sub-titles

         b. Read the first and last paragraphs

         c. Read the first sentence of all the other paragraphs

         d. THEN go back and read the entire chapter

         e. You will be SURPRISED at how this helps you understand and remember what you read

         f. NOTE: this is NOT the way that skimming is used as a shortcut instead of proper reading—it is an _____ to your reading

41. College writing follows certain CONVENTIONS. This means following accepted _____ or _____ or _____

   A. Most college writing assignments are TYPED—follow the conventions for typed papers:

      1. Font size: Use Size _____ Times New Roman

      2. Margins: Should be _____ inch all the way around:

   B. Pay special attention to the _____margin—sometimes your computer will increase that margin

   C. Typed papers in college are _____spaced

   D. Left-justified means the left-side margin is _____ except for indents and the right-side margin is _____

   E. Your name / class / date should be in the upper _____ corner

   F. Page numbers should be in the upper _____ corner—put your last name and then the number

   G. Many typed essays are now turned in electronically, but some may still be printed on paper and then turned in. Printed papers MUST be:

      1. Clean and crisp

      2. NOT wrinkled or crumpled

      3. NO soda stains or coffee stains or cat hair on them

   H. Typed essays must be the proper _____

    1. Teachers do NOT like _____ essays—it looks like you are not trying or were in a hurry:

    2. Add enough ideas and discussion to meet the minimum length requirements

    3. Teachers also do not like to read _____ essays—they have a lot of essays to read and it is more work for them:

        a. Be CONCISE in your writing

I. Avoiding ERRORS in your writing is important in college:

    1. Write in complete _____

    2. Use _____ capitalization and punctuation

    3. Use good _____ and _____

J. Your college _____ can HELP you with writing standards.

42. Homework for next time:

A. Explain a process essay—

    1. Put the pieces all together—create your ROUGH DRAFT

    2. FOLLOW the Guidelines in Section 57 on page 50

    3. Get the BEST essay you can—FOLLLOW the GUIDELINES in Session Four sections I & II; Session Five section III, Session Six section II

    4. PRINT your Final copy according to STANDARDS in the Guideline in Appendix on page 50

    5. Print 3 copies of your essay and bring to class NEXT TIME—for Peer Editing—3 COPIES typed, printed, STAPLED, and LOOKING GOOD!

B. Journal—discuss

    1. Does this way of making your Rough Draft—step-by-step—WORK for you and HELP your writing?

    2. Could you USE this technique to write OTHER college essays?

SESSION EIGHT

43. Welcome back!

    A. Journal is due—

        1. Is it LEGIBLE?

        2. Does it DISCUSS the questions B1 and B2 on previous pages?

44. Explain a process essay—

    A. Peer Editing—be a GOOD Editor—HELP them to write a GOOD essay!

    B. Follow Guidelines listed in Appendix on page 50

    C. Be a good Editor—MARK what you see!

    D. OKAY to use pencil or pen for your editing—but NO red pencil or pen!

45. Explain a process essay—what's next:

    A. Now—peer editing

    B. In 35 minutes—BIG FINISH!

    C. After class—REVIEW your essay:

        1. Peer edited copies

        2. Star copy you read yourself

    D. CONSIDER the edits and comments and make CHANGES to IMPROVE your essay

    E. Make changes and IMPROVEMENTS to turn your Rough Draft into the final copy

    F. Final copy due next time—One great copy typed / printed / stapled—to be GRADED

46. Homework—for next time

    A. Final copy due—to be graded

    B. Journal—discuss:

        1. Did the peer editing HELP you write a BETTER final copy?

        2. Are you COMFORTABLE with peer editing now?

        3. Did you see NEW THINGS when you read your star copy?

SESSION NINE

47. Welcome Back!

    A. Journal is due:

        1. LEGIBLE?

        2. Did they discuss questions on previous page in Section B?

        3. Is the journal THOUGHTFUL?

48. Using proper LANGUAGE in college is _____

    A. In college writing, there are some words you should NOT USE:

        1. Do not use _____ in your writing—find other ways to express yourself

            a. This kind of language BOTHERS or OFFENDS some readers—you do NOT want to do that!

        2. Do not use _____ in your writing

            a. It cheapens your writing and degrades the ideas you are trying to convey

        3. Do not use _____ abbreviations in your college writing

            a. In college you are writing ESSAYS, not text messages

49. In college writing, you should THINK about the _____ language you use in your writing

    A. In recent years, our society has grown more _____—the language we use needs to REFLECT that and RESPECT that

    B. What is the problem with the following words?

        1. A person who delivers mail is a MAILMAN

        2. A POLICEMAN patrols the streets to stop crime

        3. The person on the airplane who gives out snacks is a STEWARDESS

        4. At a restaurant, the WAITRESS refills your drink

    C. ALL of these words are _____ and are _____ to use.

        1. They _____ some people

        2. A substantial number of _____ are in these careers

        3. _____ people also participate in these careers

    D. Your language needs to be _____

        1. So that all people feel _____ / _____

        2. So that people do not feel _____ / _____

        3. To avoid _____ against anyone

    E. There are OTHER words you should use instead:

        1. Instead of Mailman, use _____

        2. Instead of Policeman, use _____

   3. Use_____ instead of Stewardess

   4. Use_____ instead of Waitress

F. THINK about other examples of gender usage that need to be inclusive:

   1. Salesman—use Salesperson or Account Manager instead

   2. Congressman or Congresswoman—use Member of Congress instead

   3. Chairman—use Head of the Organization or Chairperson or just Chair instead

   4. Mankind—use People or Humans instead

   5. Man-made—use Manufactured instead

G. THINK about better words you can use and FOCUS on that in your college writing

   1. You do NOT want to offend someone or HURT your own reputation—ESPECIALLY if it's unintentional!

50. Explain a Process essay—

A. Final copy due—turn it in!

   1. There is just one word to say to you: _____!

B. Writing project—what's next:

   1. Stop _____about your essay—you are DONE with it for now!

   2. After it is reviewed and checked, it will be _____ to you, and you should:

      a. _____ the comments and edits and advice

      b. _____ the changes to your essay that will improve it

      c. Be _____ about your writing—you just produced a college-level essay!

      d. Be _____ and RELIEVED that you finished such a great project!

51. Advice for the future:

A. _____

B. _____

C. _____

52. Our final class activity: our final Journal—we write it in class NOW:

A. Write your journal the same as before—a thoughtful consideration of the issues

B. One-half page or more—neat and legible

C. Discuss the following questions in your journal:

   1. What is your final reaction to the PRIME Writing program—was it worth the time and effort you put into it?

   2. Does the idea of creating your own useful workbook help you to learn and understand better? Are you going to KEEP your handbook so you can use it in the FUTURE?

   3. Was writing the Explanation essay helpful to you? Did it help you to understand concepts better by actually using them in the assignment?

   4. Do you have more CONFIDENCE in your writing abilities now?

APPENDIX
Guidelines, Reading Assignments, Worksheets, and so forth

53. Classroom expectations and standards: GUIDELINES
    A. Expectations:
        1. This course has HIGH expectations
        2. You can DO this—put forth the effort!
        3. The rewards are GREAT for you—you will BENEFIT from this course if you try!
    B. Classroom standards of behavior:
        1. We run this course the way they do in college; college standards and expectations apply:
            a. Stay alert and pay attention—no daydreaming
            b. Do the activities and assignment on time and stay up with the progress of the class
            c. Participate whenever possible in class discussions
            d. No chatting or texting in class
            e. Please leave electronic devices OFF
        2. In the event of classroom problems:
            a. You will be asked to leave the program
            b. No benefits or refunds from the program (if applicable)
54. Sentence construction worksheet:
    A. Edit the following sentences for proper construction:
    B. There may be more than one way to fix the problem
    C. NOTE: some sentences may NOT need correction—they are okay as is
    D. There is at most ONE error in each sentence—NO multiple errors
    E. Apostrophe issues:
        1. That is Johns car.
        2. My neighbour is Mr. Williams.
        3. Mr. Williams went back to the restaurant to get Mrs. Williams purse.
        4. Mr. Johnson's cat had it's kittens in our garage.
        5. Wont you please come to our party?
        6. Its the best way to mix the batter.
        7. Remove the cheese from it's package and put it in the pan.
        8. The GPS signal was not working and we got lost.

9. The dog is missing it's collar.

10. The refreshments did not arrive on time.

11. Im sorry but I couldn't make it to the meeting.

12. That wasn't the smartest thing to do.

13. Its going to rain.

14. The class was not as bad as my friend's said it would be.

F. Word choice issues:

15. There car was stolen.

16. Are you going to go their on your vacation?

17. There going to the Grand Canyon on their way home.

18. Do you know which way we need 2 go?

19. Learning to drive a stick shift requires tons of practice.

20. Do not omit the next step. It's really croosh.

21. Don't freak out if the pie crust isn't perfect the first time.

22. I have learned to except life as it is.

23. The bus full of people are late.

24. I have a strong vibe that this class will really help me out.

25. Luckily, my friend had a charger cord, and he was cool enough to let me borrow it.

26. You must rilly be careful with this next step.

27. You need to know this, for ur own good.

28. I hope the class is a member able experience.

29. Be careful so you don't mess up this next step.

30. There were defiantly some things wrong with that class.

G. Comma issues:

31. We went to the store, it was closed

32. The store was closed, we went home.

33. Apply the bronzer makeup, use the big puffy pad.

34. Jack up the car, be careful doing it.

35. Shoot the free throw, you don't want to go over the free throw line.

36. Now mix the batter, on low speed.

37. Next, add the eggs stirring the mixture while you do it.

38. Although, we were late, we still got there in time for dinner.

55. Proper form for college essays—GUIDELINES:

A. Times New Roman font is standard; some instructors want Courier New font; check with your instructor to make sure

B. Size 12 font for ALL text in the essay—NO larger font for title or headings

C. One inch margins all the way around—CHECK THIS, because the standard setting on your computer is $1\frac{1}{4}$ inch, and this makes the margins of your paper too LARGE

D. LEFT-JUSTIFIED margins; this means the left edge is straight (except for indentations) and the right edge is jagged—do NOT make the right edge straight like the left edge

E. College essays are double-spaced ALL the way through—no extra spaces above Dr below the title

F. Put proper information in the upper LEFT-hand corner—this.is all that is needed unless the instructor tells you to add more

   1. Student name—first name then last name

   2. Name of the class

   3. Date that the Assignment is being turned in—CHECK THIS: a lot of students leave it as the date they wrote the rough draft, and this in incorrect

   4. NO OTHER information is required; anything else just looks like you're trying to fill space

G. If for some reason you do include the instructor's name, make sure that it is SPELLED CORRECTLY! Many instructors take it as a personal insult when students misspell their names

H. Does the essay have a good TITLE?

   1. You do NOT have to spend three hours trying to come up with an original and impressive title, but "Paper Number Three" looks like you aren't trying very hard

   2. The title should help the reader get ready for what is coming up, but it does NOT take the place of a proper introduction, and it should be short and clear

I. Proper LENGTH of the essay.

   1. This is very important in college, so DON'T GUESS! If you are unclear about how long the paper should be, FIND OUT from yow instructor. If you cannot get a definite answer as to proper length, try to get a range of what is acceptable

   2. MAKE SURE your paper is long enough. Severe deductions in grade are made for papers that are too short

J. Proper college essay construction: intro / body / conclusion

K. Proper paragraph construction:

   1. Good flow of idea through each paragraph

   2. Good transitions between paragraphs

   3. All paragraphs about the same size

      a. Not too short, not too long

L. Good sentence construction

   1. Pay attention to grammar

   2. THINK about proper punctuation

   3. Check for proper spelling and word choice

M. Good printing presentation (if you are printing it):

   1. Clean white virgin paper

   2. Good print quality

   3. Black ink only for text

   4. If you have printer or cartridge problems, PRINT SOMEWHERE ELSE!

N. Keep your essay in PERFECT condition until you turn in:

    1. No crumpling

    2. No stains or smudges or runs

    3. Turn your essay in with PRIDE

56. Steps in the writing process:

    A. Idea gathering:

        1. Brainstorming

        2. Cloud clustering

        3. List-making

        4. Gathering notes

    B. Ensuring enough ideas and proper flow of ideas:

        1. Outlining

        2. Following and organizing notes

        3. Considering different ways of organizing your ideas

    C. Putting into proper essay form:

        1. Intro—proper introduction to bring up the topic to the reader

            a. Thesis goes in the intro—it works well as the last sentence of the intro

        2. Body—supports and elaborates on the intro

            a. Everything m the body should relate to the thesis

        3. Conclusion—echoes the intro and wraps the essay up

    D. Create a rough drafts

        1. Put all of the parts together

        2. Adjust parts of the essay for a good fit together

    E. Improve your rough draft

        1. Edit thoughts and idea for good flow

        2. Revise paragraphs and sentences for good flow and proper form

        3. Have someone else Peer Edit your essay for you

    F. Produce a good FINAL COPY:

        1. Proofread for proper sentence construction

        2. Double-check for proper layout, margins, and so forth

        3. Make sure print quality is very high

57. Explain a Process essay—ADVICE / GUIDELINES:

LAYOUT	IDEAS	MORE ADVICE
*Size 12 TNR *1-inch margins all the way *Double-spaced all the way *Left-justified margin *Name / class / date: MLA form *Page numbers: MLA form *Needs good TITLE *Proper length: three pages MINIMUM / four pages MAXIMUM *Needs proper PARAGRAPHS *Focus on good sentence construction—especially proper use of COMMAS—AVOID COMMA SPLICES *USE worksheets to help you with proper construction	* Essay form: Intro / Body / Conclusion **INTRO:** Start with GENERAL statements about your topic—TELL the reader about the topic. LEAD to thesis at END of intro—last sentence: "By following these steps . . ." then state GOAL of the process. **BODY:** In second paragraph, list ALL things needed to do the process—if necessary, TELL the reader WHERE to get the supplies needed. In third paragraph, start the process—give the STEPS in the process—but MORE is needed—in-between each step, EXPLAIN the process: Why that way / Why now / HOW to do that step / Insider tips / Advice / Encouragement / Warnings, but don't SCARE the reader **CONCLUSION:** Echo the thesis and wrap it up with POSITIVE statements— CONGRATULATIONS! YOU DID IT! and so forth	*NO "I," "me," or "my" in this essay—leave OUT *Give ALL things needed in SECOND paragraph *NO COUNTING in your steps—use OTHER transitions *Make and follow an OUTLINE to make sure the process is complete and CLEAR to the reader *Put your advice in—between each step—NOT all at the end *Be POSITIVE with your TONE—ENCOURAGE the reader!

58. Keeping a journal in college—GUIDELINES:

   A. NOT a diary—this is a READING journal

   B. Write down your THOUGHTS on the material being covered

   C. Clearly and honestly discuss what issues you see

   D. It's okay to discuss what you don't understand about the reading—after all, it's YOUR journal

   E. Handwritten journals are more direct; make sure you write clearly and legibly

   F. Some instructors in college require electronic submission of work; follow the guidelines of your instructor

59. Creative Writing: Japanese Haiku

   A. A very specific form of poetry

      1. Originally from Japan

      2. Does not have to rhyme; rhyming has nothing to do with Haiku

3. Three hoes of poetry, based on syllables:

    a. First lines is five syllables

    b. Middle line is seven syllables

    c. Last line is five syllables

4. Can be on any subject, but traditional ones often focus on peace and being in harmony with nature

B. A modest example of Haiku, written by a young student:

1. Walking through the woods

2. The sun shines down on my face

3. And makes me feel good

C. Haiku's rigid rules of construction can seem too restrictive at first, but reading and attempting to write your own Haikus can be a very enjoyable and satisfying experience